A Candle Unconsumed

poetry in the language of Jewish spirit

Rabbi Evan Schultz

Foreword by Sarah Tuttle-Singer

Vayinafash Press

Copyright ©2025 by Evan Schultz
All rights reserved. No part of this book may be used or reproduced in any manner whatsoever without written permission except in the case of brief quotations embodied in critical articles or reviews.

Published by Vayinafash Press

Vayinafash Press

Produced by GMK Writing and Editing, Inc.
Managing Editor: Katie Benoit
Copyedited by Ilana Krebs
Proofread by Katie Benoit
Text design and composition by Libby Kingsbury
Cover design by Libby Kingsbury
Printed by IngramSpark
Cover image by Shutterstock.com

Print ISBN: 978-1-966981-17-6
Ebook EISN: 978-1-966981-18-3

*Dedicated to Rabbi Arnold Sher z"l
and to all the generations of rabbis
upon whose shoulders we humbly stand*

Acknowledgments

My gratitude for this book extends both far and wide. Thank you to my friend and author Sarah Tuttle-Singer for writing the poignant foreword to this book all the way from Jerusalem. And to Gary M. Krebs who guided me through this process and made this book a reality.

I am indebted to my dear teachers over the years—Rabbi Larry Hoffman, Rabbi James Prosnit, Rabbi Danny Zemel, and Dr. Alyssa Gray—as well as my contemporary colleagues and teachers at Vayinafash—Rabbi Jill Maderer, Rabbi David Spinrad, Rabbi Judith Siegel, Rabbi Brian Stoller, Rabbi Ruth Zlotnick, Rabbi Seth Limmer, Rabbi Erica Asch, and Larry Dressler.

I hold such love and appreciation for all of my colleagues in the Tisch Fellowship, who have helped me think and write differently for the past fifteen years. Thank you to all of my study and thought partners and teachers: Rabbi Jen Gubitz, Rabbi Daniel-Bar Nahum, Rabbi Jodie Gordon, Rabbi Molly Kane, Rabbi Lyle Rothman, Rabbi Marc Katz, Rabbi Brian Immerman, Rabbi Hannah Goldstein, Rabbi Josh Beraha, Rabbi Daniel Reiser, and Betsy Stone.

To my colleagues and partners at Congregation B'nai Israel in Bridgeport—Rabbi Sarah Marion, Cantor Scott Harris, Alexa Cohen, and our entire team—I am so indebted to all of you. Thank you to the entire community at Congregation B'nai Israel. I love that each day I have the opportunity to work and dream in my beloved Jewish home.

Forever love to my family: my bold, courageous, life adventure partner and wife, Jenny Goldstein; my kids, Koby, Elie, and Roie; my parents, Linda and Fred, my sister, Alyssa; and my brother-in-law and nephew, Jon and Matthew. Remembering Ken, Carolyn, and Shirley, always.

Love to the Yenta family, Becca, Molly, Jodie, and Steph, and of course to my forever brothers, fast and firm, Adam, Matt, Keegan, Jon, Jonathan, Dan, Jon, Brett, Adrian, Aaron, Nate, and Nate.

And to my modern poetic inspirations—Rabbi Hanna Yerushalmi, Rabbi Menachem Creditor, Devon Spier, Alden Solovy, Julie Brandon—and all the Jewish poets and writers through the generations whose work moves me to write with a sense of deep love for our people and hope for tomorrow.

Thank you for buying and reading this book. I am beyond grateful to each and every one of you.

Contents

Foreword by Sarah Tuttle-Singer, xi
Introduction, 1

LOVE, 3
I'm Here to See Ecclesiastes, 5
A Prayer for All of Us, 7
Love Letters, 8
We Love You, 9
Unless it is by Love, 11
From Love, 12
Should Haves, 13
Tu B'Av, 14

ANCESTORS, 15
Within You, 16
Sunrose, Moonrose, 17
I Am, 19
Bubbe's Famous Spicy Jewishness, 22
Rainbow Tones, 23
What If, 24
Old Prophets, 25

SABBATH, 27
Before Lighting the Shabbat Candles, 29
The Unlikely, 31
Candle Meditation, 33
Sabbath Prayer, 34
On This Shabbat…, 35
The Space Between, 36
David's Harp, 37
Two Fingers, 38
For the Tired, 39
You Are Our Reason, 41

TORAH, 43
Tonight I Understood, 45
A Single Strand, 46
And It Was Good, 47

PAIN, 49
In the Dancing Wildflowers, 51
Flooding Words, 53
The Origin of Rain, 55
Birth and Loss, 56
Walking Back, 57
A Lone Sprig of Parsley, 59
The House of Comfort, 60
River Waters, 61
Too Many Weeks, 62
What-about-isms, 63

ISRAEL, 65
Four Letters at My Feet, 67
Between the Bunkers and the Sky, 69
A Missile Crashed into a Prayer, 71
Wrapped in a Ribbon, 72
The Poem Left Unwritten, 73
Modern Hebrew for Beginners, 74
Peace. Salaam. Shalom., 75
A Country of Stone, 76
Tuesday Market, 77
Notes in the Sky, 78
The Morning that Broke Me, 79
A Few Shekels and a Smile, 81

HOPE, 83
Salt from the Sky, 85
On the Day of the Eclipse, 86
Hope, Eluded, 88
Next Year, 90
Hope Met Despair, 91
Unborn Light, 92
Three Trees, 93

ONENESS, 95
Is One, 97
Anger and Sadness, 98
We are an Entire Mess, 99
This Land, 100
What is Judaism?, 101
Chanukah Oil, 102
Hidden in the Crowd, 103

LOSS, 105
The Memory Inn, 107
In Memory of Sarah Milgrim, 109
And So On, And So Forth, 111
Outlived, 112
In Memory of Hersh Goldberg-Polin, 113
One Single Word, 115
In Memory of Shiri Bibas, 116
Three Candles, 117
My Last Memory of You, 119

SPIRIT, 121
The Narrow Bridge, 123
Are. Am. Is., 124
A Candle Unconsumed, 125
Who Made Me a Jew, 127
Omer Song, 129

One More Bite of Matzah, 130
The Orchestra of Each, 131
The Day After Yom Kippur, 132

IDENTITY, 135
The Song I Did Not Compose, 137
It Was Never About, 138
My Magen, 140
You are You, 141
People of the Book, 142
People of Memory, 144
Notes, Leaves, and Letters, 145
New Years Affirmation, 146

GOD, 147
I Scheduled a Meeting with God, 149
Divine Inhalations, 151
Waiting Up, 152
The Blessing of Uncertainty, 153
Loving Parent, 154
Blueprints for Eden, 155
Americanos with an Angel, 157
A Prayer for the Prayers, 159
The Annual Chanukah Party, 160
Refunds, 161
Trick or Treat, 162
God the Painter, 163

DESIRE, 165
I Don't Want to be Heartless, 167
The Foolish Builder, 168
Psalm 151, 169
Keep Singing, 171
Yerushalmi Poems, 172
The Prophetess and the Poetess, 173

About the Author, 175

Foreword

by Sarah Tuttle-Singer

A Candle Unconsumed: Poetry in the Language of Jewish Spirit is not a book you simply READ.

It is a book you pray, weep, and wrestle with. A book you tuck into your tallit bag or your travel bag or keep next to the bed when the world feels way too loud or far too silent.

This is a book that meets you where you are and gently, insistently, lifts your face toward something extraordinary, something eternal.

To call this a book of poems would not be sufficient. Because these are not just poems—they are liturgies for our time and Midrashim of the heart and the modern age. Prayers and psalms rewritten in the margins of history, letters slipped into the cracks of war, parenthood, heartbreak, exile, and return.

They are the words we wish we had the breath to speak in hospital rooms, in bomb shelters, at Friday night dinners, and while scrolling through the headlines with a knot in our throats.

These are poems for the ones who light candles with trembling hands.

For the ones who keep dancing, even when their timbrels are broken.

For the ones who stare at the sky and ask, "Where are You?"

For the ones who ask that question into the silence—and then keep going.

The chapters unfold like movements in a great symphony of Jewish experience: Love. Ancestors. Sabbath. Torah. Pain. Israel. Hope. Oneness. Loss. Spirit. Identity. God. Desire.

Each section a meditation.

Each poem a doorway.

Each stanza a breath.

Here you'll find yourself sitting with the matriarchs at a Tel Aviv café, listening to God cry on a park bench, lighting Shabbat candles that feel more like protest than ritual. You'll find yourself wrapped in a tallit made of ash and sunlight, wandering through the wilderness with the ghosts of October 7th, braiding grief into prayer. You'll meet a God who waits up for us and then falls asleep on the couch, exhausted from all our undoing.

This book pulses with holy chutzpah—that stubborn refusal to give up on a world that keeps trying to break itself. It tells the truth about what it means to be Jewish in an age of mass mourning and messy hope. It holds both the yahrzeit candle and the havdalah flame, reminding us that, even in darkness, we still light the match.

To read these words is to remember—not just what we have lost but what we will continue to carry.

The language is intimate. Conversational. Courageous. Lyrical. Rooted in text but reaching toward something unscripted. It is unapologetically tender in a world that often mistakes cruelty for strength. It asks impossible questions and answers with metaphor, memory, and mercy.

What does it mean to live after October 7th?

What does it mean to recite "Blessed are You, who frees the captive" when captives remain?

What does it mean to count the omer while counting the names of the dead?

It means exactly what this book shows: to keep singing anyway. To build the world from love. To write Psalm 151 when no one else will. To tell the child that even if rockets fall, stars still shine.

This book is your companion through all of it—the rupture and the repair. It sits with you in the shiva tent and under the chuppah with the bride and groom. It mourns with you and dances with you. It cups your face in its hands and says, "We're still here, dear one. We're still here."

And maybe that's enough.

Maybe that's the beginning.

Introduction

One of my favorite Jewish poets, Emma Lazarus (1849–1887) wrote a piece entitled, "Gifts." In her poem, Lazarus imagines the prayers of an ancient Egyptian, Greek, Roman, and Jew. The ancient Egyptian prays for Wealth, the ancient Greek for Beauty, the ancient Roman for Power, and the Jew for Truth.

The ancient Egyptians enslaved our people for over 400 years, as described in the book of Exodus. The Greeks ransacked our ancient Temple before they were defeated by the Maccabees. And the Romans brutally destroyed the Temple in Jerusalem in the year 70 CE Despite their best efforts, those nations were unable to destroy us—or our spirit.

In her poem, Lazarus writes of the Jew that "*no fire consumes him.*" This may be a reference to the burning bush in the book of Exodus, which reads, "A messenger of God appeared to him [Moses] in a blazing fire out of a bush. He gazed, and there was a bush all aflame, yet *the bush was not consumed.*"

The metaphor of the Jew, or the Jewish people, as a perpetual flame or fire is one that has endured throughout our history. Enter any synagogue, for example, and above the Torah scrolls you will discover a *ner tamid*, an eternal light that is never to be extinguished.

We, the Jewish people, are *a candle unconsumed*. Our light and our fire has and, God-willing, will always shine brightly.

Despite all of our tragedies, from the destruction of the Temple to the pogroms to the Shoah to October 7th, our spirit has remained strong and intact. I am perpetually in awe of our people, who continue to find joy amidst the pain and love amidst the constant antisemitism and hate.

This book of poetry is an ode to that perpetual fire and incredible spirit that we continue to burn. Each section of the book—love, ancestors, Sabbath, Torah, pain, Israel, hope, oneness, loss, spirit, identity, God, and desire—are embedded in the single flame of our enduring Jewish candle.

Thank you so much for supporting and reading this book. I hope that the poems embedded within these pages help in some small way to keep the Jewish candle alive and perpetually burning.

May we, as Emma Lazarus describes, each day draw a little bit closer to Truth. May we embrace our full and joyous Jewish selves, each and every day. And may we continue to shine brightly and proudly, like a beautiful candle, unconsumed.

Am Yisrael Chai.

Love

I'm Here to See Ecclesiastes

I'm here to see Ecclesiastes.
Who?
Ecclesiastes.
She's not in right now.
Please. I need to speak with her.
I told you—
Please. She wrote me a note. It reads:
   There is a time for love, and a time for hate.
   There is a time for war, and a time for peace.
That's beautiful.
Yes.
So why do you need to see her?
I have a question.
   I need to know something before I die.
Know what?
If I will ever see that time of peace and love.
   I have seen so much war and hate.
I don't think she knows.
Well who does know?
I was hoping you humans when I created you.
Are you God?
The one and only.
Why are you working reception?
I enjoy chatting with people.
And even YOU don't know when?
   Doesn't all this war and hate bother you?
It does. I pray every day for you people.
I appreciate that.
If you want more love and peace in the world,
   that's on you.
Nobody listens.
Tell me about it.

(Continued)

I'll keep trying.
I'll keep praying.
Perhaps together we can churn out some peace.
May it be so, dear one.
Please tell Ecclesiastes I stopped by.
I will tell her.
So nice to meet you.
You too. Remember:
    Do as much as you can, dear one,
    with the precious time that you have.
    Perhaps it will be you that ushers in
    that time of peace and of love.
Amen. Amen. Amen.

A Prayer for All of Us

Creator of hands and heart,
we sing a fractured song.
The eyes of your beloved children
have hardened like ice;
so much so that we
barely still see
the immeasurable divinity
in one another's tired faces.

Where are you?
Help us.
Be by our side
as the chasm between us
widens and grows
nearly beyond
what a bridge can span.

Be our loving parent,
hold our wounds,
sing us the song
we alone cannot write.
Show us the path
we cannot see
on our own.

Create us anew
like the first flowers of spring.
Help us to sing
whole notes
and hymns of hopefulness.
Imbue within us
the hands and the heart
of wholeness and peace.

Love Letters

Tonight
I wrote you
a love letter,
to catch
your
inconsolable
tears
as you
sit
and wait
with the
voiceless moon,
humming
frayed prayers and
splintered psalms

for your
children
to return
home
from the
empty
wilderness

with a
love letter
in their
wounded
hand
to catch
your
joyful tears.

We Love You

Yesterday I saw

Sarah
 Rebecca
   Leah &
   Rachel

sitting at a cafe,
sipping espressos
and laughing together!

Excuse me I said
are you…?

Yes! They replied.
We are

Laughter
 Kindness
   Strength &
    Power

I've read about you—
I'm your—

And just like that
they were gone.

On the table
they left a note.

(Continued)

May the One who
blessed us,
bless you
with laughter,
kindness, strength
and power
dear one.
Even in the most
difficult of days.
We love you.

As I walked away
I softly smiled,
holding my
ancestors'
prayer
tightly in my
hand,
knowing they
are with me,
always.

Unless it is by Love

who by fire
who by shooting

these are not just words
from the prayerbook

they are our reality

please please no more
who by

unless it is by love.

From Love

Abba, can you play that song
just one more time before—

Before what, my child?

Before the world goes to sleep
and rockets turn to stars.

My song is a song of peace,
and I will one day pass it to you.

But what if I live to see peace?
What becomes of the song?

The song will be gently buried
beneath the ancient city stones.

And as the child drifted to sleep
her father dreamt for her and sang:

You will build this world from love.
You will build this world, from love.

Inspired by my friend Rabbi Menachem Creditor.

Should Haves

For texting when I should have called.
For listening when I should have heard.
For waiting when I should have started.
For fearing when I should have spoken.
For missing what I should have seen.
For watching when I should have come.
For asking when I should have realized.
For being when I should have acted.
For shouting when I should have spoken.
For keeping what I should have given.
For preaching what I should have lived.
For ignoring what I should have noticed.
For going when I should have waited.
For doubting when I should have believed.
For all these and more, I ask forgiveness.

Tu B'Av

Tonight is Tu B'av.
What's that?
It's like Jewish
 Valentine's Day.
I see.
Minus the expensive
 three course dinners.
So what do you do then?
Tell people
 you love them.
That's it?
That's it.
No chocolate?
Well if you want.
No cards?
Thank goodness no.
Sounds awesome.
yep no Hamans
 or Pharaohs.
Just love.
Just love.
Sounds pretty perfect.
I love you.
I love you too.

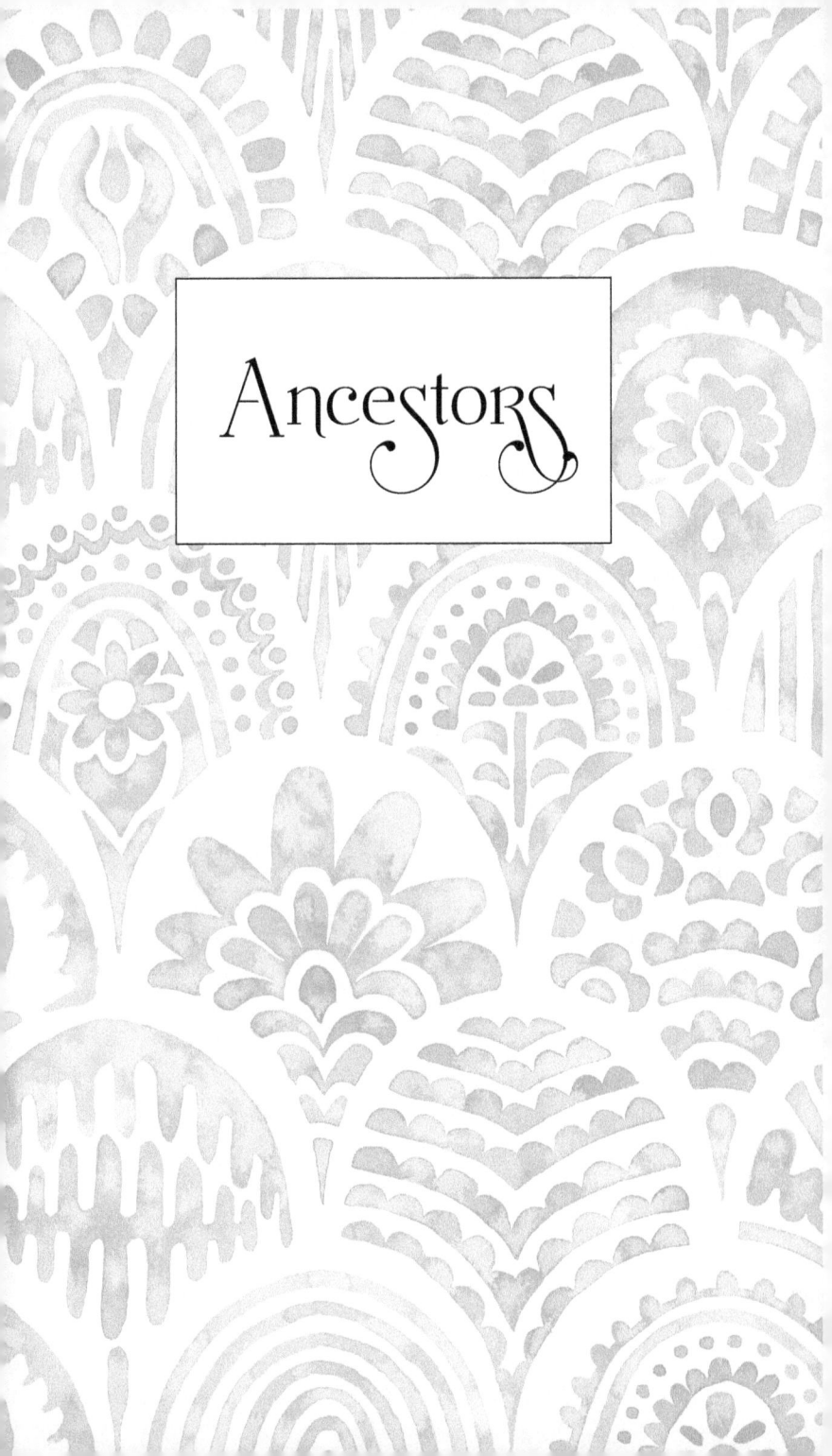

Ancestors

Within You

Within you dwells
the laughter of Sarah
the faithfulness of Abraham
the kindness of Rebecca
the curiosity of Isaac
the boldness of Leah
the persistence of Rachel
the imperfection of Jacob
the foresight of Joseph
the humility of Moses
the well of Miriam
the heart of Aaron
the courage of Joshua
the poetry of David
the wisdom of Solomon
the voice of Vashti
the leadership of Esther
the longing of Ruth
the pain of Job
the justice of Isaiah
the goodness of Micah
the decisiveness of Deborah
the love of Amos
the creativity of the divine.

Sunrose, Moonrose

At sunrise this morning
I took my coffee and
drove to the shores
of the sea of reeds

where my mother
danced with Miriam
and my father quietly
wept away the bitterness.

There I found remnants
of a broken timbrel
and the torn pages
of an ancient siddur

so I took the timbrel
in my hand
and silently danced
for a while upon the sand.

And as the moon rose and
the tide shifted away
I planted the pages
gently within the earth.

I quietly wondered if
that sea would
ever part again
for others who cry.

(Continued)

And just then as I set
my foot in the salty water
the sea miraculously
began to open up

leading me to the land of tears
where i took out my mother's timbrel
and recited from memory
the prayers of my father.
And hearing their cries,
I lifted them up
and brought them home
through the parted waters of the sea.

I Am

I am
songs of peace
late nights at summer camp
Israeli dancing
and Sabbath joy.

I am
knishes on Delancey
Sammy's Roumanian
the streets of jerusalem
and matzah ball soup.

I am
Shema
Yisrael
havdalah by the lake
blasts of the shofar
and the hora.

I am
klezmer music
Debbie Friedman
pursuing justice
and Shabbos dinners.

I am
Emma Lazarus
Miriam's cup
let my people go
and Manischewitz.

(Continued)

I am
am Yisrael chai
love your neighbor
Marc Chagall
and the mourners Kaddish.

I am
Abraham Joshua Heschel
Chanukah candles
Leonard Cohen
and the sea of Talmud.

I am
questions not answers
Golda Meir
Sabbath candles
and Torah queries.

I am
Sarah Silverman
beit mitzvah parties
sunrise masada
and people of the book.

I am
standing at Sinai
challah french toast
Bubbe's kugel
and Sarah's laughter.

I am
Cynthia Ozick
Elie Wiesel
Fiddler on the Roof
and the six million.

I am
bearer of tradition
keeper of my faith
proud of who i am
and never afraid.

This is who I am.
L'chayim
L'chayim
L'chayim.

Bubbe's Famous Spicy Jewishness

2 tsp Queens, NY
3 tbsp Lower East Side
 (before it was hip)
3 tbsp Catskills
1 cup Yiddish (ya putz!)
1 box matzah (in the kitchen
 twelve months a year)
3 tsp Ashkenazi Hebrew
 (Bar'chu es Adonay)
3 tbsp removable car radio
2 cups Neil Diamond's
 "Coming to America"
1 copy of *The Jazz Singer*
1 copy of *Yentl*
1 cup blaming Zayde for
 everything
4 tbsp never again
3 cups matzah ball soup
1 pinch kvetching
2 pinches kvelling
(maybe reverse those)
1 light, never to go out.

Rainbow Tones

Our palette was once filled with
vivid and wild rainbow tones
like Joseph's coat of many colors.

And slowly, oh so painfully slowly,
the colors began to dilute and mix
with salt and sand from the wild.

Blue turned to the color of stone,
green morphed into mortar,
and purple, a fallen nova star.

Left with only shades of orange,
I now paint gentle brushstrokes
of memory, hope, and life.

What If

What if God
had asked Sarah
to go forth?

One who cried
for her children,
rather than one
who was willing
to sacrifice his?

Oh, how the world
might be different.

Old Prophets

I heard that
Isaiah, Amos, and
Jeremiah
were in town.

I found them
at the local
watering hole
four whiskeys in.

I introduced
myself and said
I'm a huge fan
of your work.

They laughed
and told me
to forget about
justice and streams

nobody listens
to old prophets,
as they took
another swig of
the bottle of
love and regret.

I paid their tab
and walked home.

(Continued)

Old prophets may
lose hope,
but mine will endure
like an unfailing stream.

Before Lighting the Shabbat Candles

This week,
may these candles
become more than a
source of
magnificent light.

This week,
may these candles
become more than a
marker of
sacred time.

This week,
may these candles
become
a shared vision.
A collective prayer.
A human hope.

Two candles
dwelling
side by side
one light no greater
than the other.

A vision of equality
and equity in
our cities and our towns
crafted by those who
care deeply
for the fate
of others.

(Continued)

A prayer for peace
and coexistence
between those who
war and hate
and fight over
and over
and over
and over again.
For what?

A hope for a world
one day
redeemed
where
human beings
are each
celebrated and seen
in God's sacred image.

This week,
two candles.
a shared vision.
A collective prayer.
A human hope.
For our children
and our children's children.
And even perhaps,
for us.

Blessed are you
source of strength
and inspiration
who prompts us to
kindle
the Sabbath lights.

The Unlikely

the challah is unbraided
the candles unlit.
the wine is unpoured
the table unset.

the guitar is unplayed
the song is unsung.
the sabbath bride is unwed
the hungry children unfed.

the future unknown
the world is unjust.
the soul is unlocked
the heart is unsewn.

the questions unasked
the hands still unheld.
the beauty unseen
the peace still unmet.

there is still time to undo
all that is undone.
to release the unfree
and quiet the unrest.

to craft the unbuilt
to express the unsaid.
to stir the unmoved
to love the unwilling.

(Continued)

to hold the uncertain
to believe that unless.
to write the untitled
to wildly dream the unlikely.

Candle Meditation

Tonight I light
two candles.

One
for my
heartbreak
mourning
grief
longing
brokenness.
Shevarim!

And one
for my
wholeness
pride
love
joys
strength.
Tkiyah!

I am broken
and I am whole.
I am shvarim
and I am
tkiyah.

I am
two candles.
Still shining.
Always shining.

Sabbath Prayer

May those who hold pain
find spaces of soulful healing.

May those who carry sadness
find sweetness in holy jars of honey.

May those who are wildly tired
find the timely gift of breath and rest.

May those who feel emptiness
find the wellspring of replenishment.

May those who feel vulnerable
find the sanctuary of divine-like wings.

May those who feel loneliness
find nourishment from human love.

And may those who feel hopeless
find the sparks of radical goodness.

May we all strengthen one another.
Shabbat Shalom.

On This Shabbat...

On this Shabbat,
may my heart find reprieve,
may my neshama find breath,
may my neighbors find love,
may my children find safety,
may my people find comfort,
may my hands find creativity,
may my words find acceptability,
may my ears find melodious melody,
may my feet find firm ground,
may my prayers find realization,
may my soul find wholeness,
may my eyes find stillness,
may my mind find openness,
may my mouth find lots of smiles,
may my cup find sweetness,
may my world find reconciliation,
and may my days find meaning.

The Space Between

The space between
Jewish pain
and
Jewish joy
is
Jewish presence.

And that
is where
I find myself

as
Shabbat
unites
with my
weary
Jewish soul.

David's Harp

I found David's ancient harp
in a half-stale cereal box
as my children ran past
and the newspaper awaited
my daily sighs and tears.

It hadn't been played
since the air was sweeter,
the chords of a poet
who wailed upon the stones
and turned friendship to love.

My dry, tired hands touched
the frail and fragile strings
and behold! the Sabbath
enveloped the entire earth,
a brief eternity, of peaceful song.

Two Fingers

If on Sabbath eve
you find yourself
lost in the dark
take your two fingers
become the candles
and light the way.

For the Tired

For the tired,
the deeply tired—
tired from jobs
election ads
family illness
ongoing war
daily heartaches
deep worries
and anxieties.

May you find
vayinafash—
deep refreshment
and nourishment
of the spirit
and of the soul,
even if just for
a single moment
on the seventh day,
to be still,
to listen,
and to find rest.

You deserve rest.
To remove the
weight from
your shoulders,
to close your
weary eyes,
to calm your
fatigued hands.

(Continued)

On this Shabbat—
you dear soul,
so very tired,
tired from so much,
may you
on this day
find a moment
of true rest,
nourishment
refreshment,
vayinafash.

You Are Our Reason

The Sabbath bride
did not show up
for L'cha Dodi.

The congregation stood
waiting, staring
at the sanctuary door.

First they waited
for a few minutes.
Then hours.
Days. Weeks. Years.

Until finally one Shabbat,
the doors creaked open.

The Sabbath bride appeared.

The music resumed.
Yai lai lai L'cha Dodi!
the congregation sang,
now years older,
their legs tired,
their souls aged.

All those years,
they waited.

Just to sing.
To finish the song.

(Continued)

You needn't wait for me
to sing beautiful songs,
said the bride.

The people began to cry.
Some days, they said,
we need reason to sing.

You are our reason.

And from that day forward,
the Sabbath bride returned
every Friday night,
so even during the most
difficult of weeks
the people had reason
to sing.

Torah

Tonight I Understood

Tonight I
understood
why our
scrolls

have no
commas
or periods

for our
story
is
one loooooong run on sentence

each letter
a life
a song
a generation
a blessing

punctuated
only
by love
and
by light.

A Single Strand

I found a single strand from a tallit this morning at the synagogue.
It must have accidentally fallen off.
Now there's a prayer shawl out there with only 612 knots and fringes.
One mitzvah missing. Fallen.
I wonder which one.
Love your neighbor?
Welcome the stranger?
Justice, justice you shall pursue?
Whichever it may be, what an image of what it means to repair the world.
To reattach the missing string.
To mend what we've broken.
How empowering to know that we each hold the missing string in our hands.
We just have to figure out how to reattach it.

And It Was Good

On the first day
God created my heart
so that I could
love my neighbor
and it was good.

On the second day
God created my breath
so that I could
pulse with the waves
and it was good.

On the third day
God created my hands
so that I could
craft and sculpt and build
and it was good.

On the fourth day
God created my soul
so that I could
be uniquely me
and it was good.

On the fifth day
God created my feet
so that I could
humbly walk the earth
and it was good.

On the sixth day
God created my mind
so that I could
speak for what is just
and it was good.

On the seventh day
God and I rested
so that we could
sing a song of gratefulness
and it was very good.

Pain

In the Dancing Wildflowers

I swim
alone
through
the sea of
three
dimensional
transient
rain.

The
pangs
of confusion
coursing
through
my
broken
heart.

A child
extends
her hand
and
offers the
sun.

And for
a brief
moment
I look
up
and

(Continued)

with a
softened
smile

I let go
of
my pain
and
see
peace
in the
dancing
wildflowers.

Flooding Words

And God saw
the universe was
flooding
with words.

Angry words.
Hateful words.
Racist words.
Antisemitic words.
Ignorant words.
Fearful words.
Bigoted words.
Nonsensical words.
Lying words.
Narrow-minded words.
Twisted words.
Hurtful words.
Shameful words.
Fighting words.
Small-minded words.
Disgusting words.
Spiteful words.
Vicious words.

So God built
for Herself
an ark.

(Continued)

For 40 days
and 40 nights
She waited.
And waited.
And waited.

Until one day
the flooding words
finally evaporated
far away
into the sky.

The Origin of Rain

Some people say
that rain
is God's tears.

But perhaps
the rain
was once
the tears
from our
very eyes.

Collected
over time by
the rivers
and the oceans.
Lifted to the sky
and absorbed
by the clouds.

The rain is
our own tears,
not God's.
Showering us
in past sadness
and future
joys and hopes.

Birth and Loss

On Rosh Hashanah
we celebrate the
birth of the world.

On Tisha B'av
we mourn the
loss of our holy place.

On Tu Bishvat
we celebrate the
birth of the trees.

On Yom Hashoah
we mourn the
loss of the six million.

On Passover
we celebrate the
birth of our people.

On Yom Hazikaron
we mourn the
loss of our heroes.

On Yom Haatzmaut
we celebrate the
birth of our homeland.

A cycle of birth and loss,
celebration and mourning.

A Jewish year
in all its poignant beauty.

Walking Back

After crossing the sea

one Israelite
saw the dancing
and the singing.

He immediately
turned around
and began walking back.

Where are you going?
they asked
with their timbrels
high in the air.

My whole life
I have known
only pain, he said.

I do not know
how to dance
or how to sing.

So they took his hand
and offered him joy.

And he cried into the sea.
He danced away some of the pain.
He sang the sweetest song.

It is those very tears
we cry at every
Jewish simcha to this day.

It is that very dance
we perform at every
Jewish festival to this day.

And it that very song
we sing any time
we want to turn around
and go back.

The song of joy.
The song of hope.

A Lone Sprig of Parsley

To be a Jew is
to see ourselves
as the lone
sprig of parsley
swimming in a sea
of saltwater.

The House of Comfort

I found my way to a synagogue.
There were three doors.
The house of comfort.
The house of joyfulness.
And the house of return.
I entered the house of comfort.
And there I found
exactly what I sought.

River Waters

it takes years
for river waters
to soften stones.

how much
the more so
to soften hearts.

Too Many Weeks

On week 1, I mourned.
On week 2, I cried.
On week 5, I waited.
On week 7, I hoped.
On week 12, I sang.
On week 18, I sat down.
On week 25, I lamented.
On week 28, I prayed.
On week 31, I shouted.
On week 34, I believed.
On week 39, I grieved.
On week 41, I screamed.
On week 43, I wept.
On week 46, I longed.
On week 50, I wished.

What-about-isms

Last night I dug a hole
deep into the ground.
And in it I placed all
of our callousness
and what-about-isms
and misguided absurdity.

As I shoveled the earth
and filled in the pit,
a passing stranger stopped
and handed me a seed.

Place that on top she said.

And together we prayed,
two strangers under the moon,
that from that very spot
something beautiful would grow.

Four Letters at My Feet

A missile
shot right
through
my prayer
for peace.

The letters
shin ש
lamed ל
vav ו
mem ם
fluttered
to my feet.

I fell
to my
knees
and I
cried
alongside
those four
fallen
letters.

Tomorrow
I will awaken
and gather
them up
in my hands
and
stubbornly

(Continued)

try again.
And I will sing
oseh
shalom
bimromav
may the One
who makes
peace in
the heavens
tomorrow
hear
our prayers
for peace
one day
in Jerusalem.

Between the Bunkers and the Sky

My words,
my prayers,
feel garbled,
confused

like strings
of a guitar
twisted and
tied, braided
all together.

There's so much
I want
to say.
Pray.

About being
a Jew.

About what
feels lost.
Or gone.

About what
could be.

But like I said—
they are somewhere
between the
bunkers and
the sky.

(Continued)

So for now
I'll just sing
baruch Atah Adonai—
blessed are You

who placed me
in this moment
with garbled
silent prayers

a clear heart
and open hands

and there is
so much
I can do
with that.

A Missile Crashed into a Prayer

It was reported on the news
that a missile crashed
into a prayer.

Nothing was left of the prayer.
All the letters and words
destroyed. Gone.

It was a child's prayer.
She launched it to the sky
before falling asleep.

Witnesses report
it was a prayer for peace.

There will be no shiva.

Wrapped in a Ribbon

My Judaism is wrapped
in a yellow ribbon.

I count the days.
I know their names.
How many remain.

I recite prayers
that I hope expire.

A number taped
to a shirt.
Days since that day.

My ribbon is frayed.
But not my hope.

The Batman logo
will never be the same.

My song is
bring them home.
Oseh Shalom.

Blessed are You,
who frees the captive.

The Poem Left Unwritten

The poem left unwritten,
its author impatiently awaits
the messiah's urgent phone call

and as she sits and anxiously toils
the ink on her pen dries up,
her words kidnapped by despair

she is left to bewail to the sky
about failures and frustrations
as she recites the Kaddish once more

for soldiers and children's children
buried alongside her unwritten verses
by the still calm shores of the sea

where footprints once danced
and we asked "who is like You?"
with timbrels and melancholy hope

glistening like glitter upon sand
our ancestors dreamed of the poet
who would one day write the song

that could harmonize the universe
and when she does we can say
excuse me, my phone is finally ringing.

Modern Hebrew for Beginners

ahava, love.
tikvah, hope.
chesed, kindness.
emet, truth.
shleymut, wholeness.
olam, world.
lev, heart.
tov, goodness.
rachamim, compassion.
or, light.

Peace. Salaam. Shalom.

The stone spoke to the tree
as the moon sang to the earth,
may we share the space
above and beneath the heavens?

The tree offered the etchings
of the branches and leaves,
as the rock gifted the edges,
contours and craggy curves.

The moon painted the light
of the wild galaxies upon them,
as the earth received
the imprints of angelic travelers.

And as the humans gazed
at their concrete wilderness,
the rock, earth, tree, and moon
made peace, salaam, shalom.

A Country of Stone

Israel is a country of stone.
Jagged, sharp, piercing,
harsh, wild, and rough.

I picture an artist, weeping,
brushstrokes across the stones,
year after year after year.

The tragic hues of red marry
the white, pink, and cream
of the ancient and modern.

I walk bare upon the stones,
like the tops of mountains
their stories pierce my soft feet.

It is then that Abraham and Sarah
appear to wash my punctured soles
like I am an angel at their door.

The water for a brief moment
softens the rigidness of the stone
where voices cry from below.

I take the pitcher of my ancestors
and wash the feet of another,
two angels of hope, atop the stone.

Tuesday Market

On Tuesdays there is
an artist's market
in the city of Tel Aviv

where one can buy
havdalah sets and
colorful paintings,
ceramics, and hamsas.

They don't sell rockets
or hand grenades there,
just works of the crafter
and blessings of creativity

for tourists to take home
and show their friends,
this is the Israel I know,
colorful, fragile, and miraculous.

Notes in the Sky

If I could I'd fire a music note
far across the enemy lines
into trembling bomb shelters
and nurseries void of lullabies.

Guitar strings would awaken
the slumbering soldiers
and they'd dance wildly about,
as cellos and violins would
drown out shouts of
readies, aims, and fires.

If only a music note could
mesmerize an army captain
and sprout a song of peace,
I'd be the first to launch it
deep into the wounded sky.

The Morning that Broke Me

October 7.
That morning broke me.
Into 1,200 pieces.
I will never forget it.
I ran to check on my kids.
It was Simchat Torah.
We still held services.
We didn't know the extent.
The scrolls unraveled.
The music shattered.
Nova.
Be'eri.
Nir Oz.
Adonai oz l'amo yitein.
God weeps.
I call to the angel of peace.
I think about the hostages.
Every day.
Hersh. Eden. Ariel.
A one-year-old baby.
Bring them home.
Why are they not home?
I'm worried.
I'm scared.
I'm proud.
A narrow bridge.
Do not be afraid.
My people are wounded.
But yes, still alive.
Two candles flicker.
I'm out of prayers.

(Continued)

So I just cry.
I'm out of tears.
So I just gaze.
At the morning news.
At the sky.
At their photographs.
As I kiss my children.
I've dreaded this day.
One year.
Shiva eternal.
Still broken.
Held together with hope.
And wild dreams.
And honey so sweet.
Such is my lot.
My people live on.
Tikvateinu.
Dancing again.
On the shores of the sea.
Almost. Forever.
Release.
Hold on.
Zichronam livracha.
Remember them.
Be a blessing.
Go forth, to life.

A Few Shekels and a Smile

Years ago I wandered into
a used book palace
on a dreamlike street
in the heart of
the city of Jerusalem

where bins of prayerbooks
aged gracefully
waiting to be adopted
by a hopeful soul
walking on their way

and it just so happened
that hopeful soul
was a younger version of me
looking for the lyrics
to a tattered old song

so I handed the owner
a few shekels and a smile
someone else's old prayers
now mine to sing softly with
the dreamers of Jerusalem.

Hope

Salt from the Sky

Salt from the sky
as Lincoln's song
evokes empty rain
from my fractured spirit.

I stare at a photograph
of what once stood
as my child hugs me
and asks why.

The salt turns to hail,
a friend's melody prompts
heart filled meditations
and my mouth to speak.

But today I have no words
no meditations of the heart,
only bittersweet gazes
and quiet prayers of peace.

On the Day of the Eclipse

On the day of the eclipse
an angel handed God
a pair of
special glasses.

This is for looking down
toward the earth,
the angel told God.

When God looked down
God saw
all the people looking up!
smiling, crying
wearing the
exact same glasses.

Today
they are in the
rare path of totality,
the angel told God.

And us?
God asked the angel.

Today
said the angel,
we are in the
rare path of humanity.

And in that moment
God and the angel also
gently smiled and cried,

praying it would
last an eternity.

Hope, Eluded

I have days
when hope
eludes me.

When the
ocean
tides pull
so strenuously
at my feet
they nearly
knock me
to the
sand.

It's in
those hours
I look
quietly
to the
mountains

and lovingly
say to
my heart
tomorrow
the world
will be
created anew

and as
I arise
I softly
pray

hope
will
embrace
me once
again.

Next Year

The two
most poignant
words
in the entire
seder
are
"next year."

Hope Met Despair

Hope met despair
on a quiet Sunday night
in an open, faraway field
beneath the wild sky

hope was exhausted,
despair told her
not to fade away
into the chaos of humanity

and so they held hands
deep into the night
where hope could briefly rest
upon despair's fragile heart.

Unborn Light

A stranger asked me

why dear friend
do you kindle
two lights each
Sabbath night?

There are places,
worlds,
hearts,
and souls,
I replied
where there is yet
to be light.

Unborn light.

And maybe
ever maybe…

Those sabbath flames
just might
bring light
to the darkest
worlds,
places,
hearts,
and souls.

And that,
I said,
dear stranger,
is what we call hope.

Three Trees

This morning I saw three trees.
One had lost all its leaves.
One was left with half its leaves.
One still carried all its leaves.

It was comforting to know
that beneath the earth
their roots intertwine,
sharing nourishment and life.

So may it be for all of us.

Oneness

Is One

Shema
   listen.
   hold the space.
   breathe in.
   hear.
Yisrael
   to my song.
   and the questions.
   our people.
   our cry.
Adonai
   merciful one.
   divine spirit.
   my rock.
   my well of hope.
Eloheinu
   our voice.
   our creativity.
   breathe out.
   our strength.
Adonai
   my melody.
   my spaciousness.
   my breath.
   my pain.
Echad.
   is one.
   is one.
   is one.
   is one.

Anger and Sadness

Anger and sadness
divided the world in two.

And for centuries,
nearly eternity,
the two never met.

Half the world was angry,
and half the world was sad.

Until one day a child
took a paintbrush
in her tiny little hand

and mixed the two

like mixing blue and red
to create purple,

anger and sadness mixed
to create peace.

And on that day,
on that singular day,
You became One.

We are an Entire Mess

You
Are
An
Entire
World.

We
Are
An
Entire
Mess.

But
Sometimes
Messiness
Leads
To
Creation.

Creation
Leads
To
New
Beginnings.

New
Beginnings
Begin
With
Us.

This Land

This land is our land
from the L.A. wildfires
to the Florida hurricanes
to the Texas blizzards
to the Asheville storms
to the Tennessee tornadoes
to the Vermont floods.

This land needs you and me
to heal it one hand at a time.

What is Judaism?

Some say Judaism
is a people, an ethnicity
a religion, a nation
even a conversation.

But to me,
Judaism is a soul.

Chanukah Oil

Why a holiday centered around oil?
What element better represents the Jewish people?
Oil can hold the light, for longer than anyone ever expected.
Oil can take the heat, when things are tough, it endures.
Oil is messy, and let's just say being Jewish is always messy.
What better symbol to represent who we are.

Hidden in the Crowd

We debate what we cannot control.
We avoid what we don't understand.
We laugh at the discomfort.
We swim along with the pain.
We question what exists.
We listen for the answers.
We grieve an innocent stranger.
We fear what we might learn.
We argue over dinner.
We lie in bed awake.
We pretend we're not worried.
We pray to an absent God.
We hide in the crowd.
We still believe in hope.
We still build this world, from love.

Loss

The Memory Inn

Last night I visited
the memory inn
deep within the forest
of grief, sorrow,
birds, flowers, and trees.

It was there I saw
majestic trunks
fallen, kissing the earth
their still silhouettes
the home of newfound life.

Cracked, quiet branches
feed and nourish the
birds and amphibians,
plants and flowers,
the beetles and the bugs.

And as I sat and cried for them
a living tree whispered to me
dear human please understand
when you come to pass
like a beautiful, fallen tree

You too will return to
lie among the forest floor
to instill new life and growth
into children's eyes and
mourners broken hearts.

(Continued)

And they will hold you close
like the tree upon the forest floor
your song feeding their souls
like the sweet birds and flowers
here within the memory inn.

Written in memory of Paul Kane, z"l.

In Memory of Sarah Milgrim

Yitzhak Rabin met
Sarah Milgrim
in heaven.

She was in tears.

You and I, we
drew too close
to the well of peace,
he said softly,
trying to offer
her comfort.

And why does
that frighten people?
she asked.

Some only thrive
in brokenness,
he answered.

Now what?
she asked,
as her tears
fell to the earth.

The angels
gathered around them
and held them.

(Continued)

We pray, he said,
as he took a song
from his pocket.

We pray that
there is another
Sarah out there.

And as they bowed
their heads

they could hear
the still, soft
voices below

reciting her name,
singing the melodies
of memory and peace.

And So On, And So Forth

A child of four
taken from home
lives among
the faraway fields
and hides up
in the sky
when they come
to take him away.
And so on, and so forth.

A child of five
lost among the trees
his parents
recite the Kaddish
for aunts and uncles
of blessed memory
as he barely lives
among the barely living.
And so on and so forth.

A child of six
arrested for unknown
from barracks to barns
as trains fly him
to the fragile safety
of the kindest stranger
his uncle somehow sings
our sweetest of songs.
And so on, and so forth.

Dedicated to all those who perished in the Shoah, the Holocaust, and those few who survived and live to this day to tell their stories.

Outlived

We are outlived by the trees
and by the elder stones,
by the autumn leaves
and the brightest moon.

We are outlived by the sky
and by the dancing rivers,
by the wildflowers
and by the ancient timber.

We are outlived by the stories
and by the tales,
by the nighttime melodies
and by the prayers.

We are outlived by the past
and the ever present,
by the aspirations
and by the generations.

We are outlived by creation
and by unfinished journeys,
by our good names
and the sweet honeybees.

We are outlived by eternity
and fluttering doves,
by our precious teachings
and all who we loved.

In Memory of Hersh Goldberg-Polin

Queen Esther met
Hersh Goldberg-Polin
at the heavenly
Purim celebration.

Unto our people
there was light
she recalled to him
as he gently nodded.

There still is light, he said—
my mom and my dad…
his voice trailed off.
They were my light.

You were their light,
she said softly.

Just then they heard
a roar of boos
from earth below.

Haman.

The people need light.

So Esther and Hersh
began to sing,
Unto our people
there was light
may it be so for us
may it be so for us.

(Continued)

The boos ceased.
They put their ears
to the clouds.
They heard joy.

And for the first time
they smiled
and there was light.

One Single Word

Tradition teaches us that
before we are ready to be born,
we possess infinite knowledge,
the innermost secrets of Torah.

And in my lifetime I have seen
that just before we die,
we utter one single word
that ascends high into the air.

As for the space in between,
we try to regain what was lost
and breathe in the disparate words
to craft eternal songs of loving memory.

Dedicated to the memories of Shiri, K'fir, and Ariel Bibas. May their memories be a forever blessing.

In Memory of Shiri Bibas

Rabbi Akiva met
Shiri Bibas in heaven.

How did you die?
she asked the sage.

I died at the hands
of the Romans.
My final words
were words of love.

How about you?
he asked kindly.

I died at the hands
of Hamas.

My final words
were words of love.

Little has changed
they cried.
So little, for our people,
has ever changed.

Three Candles

The yartzeit candle
kindles our past
our ancestors
our memories
the eternal flame
the quiet tears
I miss them
the innocents lost
our thread of grief
yitgadal v'yitkadash
within that flame
we remember them.

The sabbath candles
kindle our present
our daily dance
opposites and pairs
you and I
this and that
us and them
two lovers
two not yet one
the space between
l'hadlik ner
I am awake to today.

The havdalah candle
kindles our future
two become one
enmeshed
embracing
the world whole

(Continued)

a singular song
the audacity of peace
one flame
ken tihyeh lanu
may it be for us
like a braided candle.

My Last Memory of You

After you died I needed to understand.

So I went to a sage and asked,
help me please to understand.

The sage sat down next to me
and offered me the gift of presence.

But I did not understand.

Then I went to an angel and asked,
help me please to understand.

The angel gracefully encircled me
and sang to me a precious song.

But I did not understand.

Then I went to see to the divine
and asked to help me understand.

The divine cried innumerable tears
and gently held my cracked soul.

And as I was held by God,
listening to the angel's song,
in the presence of the sage,

I turned to my last memory of you,
letting it fully encircle my body
like a spell of swarming grief,

(Continued)

until I was ready to quietly go,
held by angels and loving sages,
less and less needing, to understand.

Spirit

The Narrow Bridge

The narrow bridge calls to me:
Do not be afraid!

My bare feet rest upon
her ancient timber planks
which match the vibrant colors
of the woven prayer shawl

that envelops my soul
on sabbath mornings
as I pray poetic words
I don't yet understand.

There at the very locus
of the bridge I wait,
I am the spitting image of
my Zayde's ancient shield.

My life is interlocking triangles
encased by two blue lines
like the parallel bars
I am a gymnast holding pose

She calls to me once more
as I tarry for all my days,
upon the narrow bridge
looking up, never afraid.

Are. Am. Is.

In Hebrew there's no word for "are," "am," or "is."
Our existence is part of our very identity.
"Ani" means I am. "Anachnu," we are.

It is the invisible, connecting spirit.
The space between the letters of Torah.
That which we pass on to our children.

Even in the throes of the wilderness.
And when we dance the hora.
Whatever happens to us, it can't be taken away.

We are. We, God willing, always will be.

A Candle Unconsumed

A rabbi went to visit
the arsonist.

She sat before him.
Unafraid.
Like Miriam. Like Ruth.

She brought forth
two unlit candles,
placing them before him.

You see, she said,
we are the people
of fire and light.

The eternal flame.
The bush unconsumed.
The braided fire.

You cannot destroy us
with what keeps us alive.

She lit the two candles.
She recited a blessing.
She prayed for peace.

And as she stood to leave,
she could see the man
watching in awe

as the candles burned,
unconsumed.

(Continued)

Written in memory and honor of the victims of the attack on the Boulder, Colorado, Run for Their Lives group attacked in June 2025.

Who Made Me a Jew

Some of our prayers feel so difficult to recite lately.
The words, unrealized.

Blessed are You, who frees the captives.
Blessed are You, who blesses us with peace.
Blessed are You, who lifts up the fallen.

I tell myself these are aspirational,
not descriptions of the present.
So I recite them—with weariness.

But then I see the prayer,
Blessed are You, who has made me a Jew.

For this, I should thank God?
My people are literally being burned alive.
And shot down in the streets.

Yes, I tell myself, for this, I am still thankful.

Because it is how God created me.
And how I wake up each morning
and lie down to sleep each evening.

It is my daily call to pursue justice,
love my neighbor, welcome the stranger,
live with curiosity and smile with wonder.

It is my Bubbe and my Zayde,
my parents and my children,
my people, my pride, my soul.

(Continued)

Thus even on the most difficult days,
I speak these words of gratitude
for making me who I am.

Omer Song

To count the memories,
the blessings, and the sunrises.

To count the weddings,
the births, and the sunsets.

To count the hugs,
the phone calls, the laughter.

To count the friends,
the journeys, and the stories.

To count the loves,
the sweetness, and the sky.

To count the illnesses,
the prayers, and the raindrops.

To count the get-togethers,
the wishes, and the dreams.

To count the days,
the moments, and the gifts.

To count is to be human.
To count is to be present.
To count is to remember.

One More Bite of Matzah

A sink full of dirty dishes
empty bottles of grape juice
we ate all the matzah ball soup
wine stains on the tablecloth
matzah crumbs on the floor
unopened Dr. Brown's
late night storytelling
a messy pile of haggadahs
half filled seltzer bottles
no more room in the fridge
seder noise faded into the night
children fall asleep too late
what do we do with the shank bone
one more bite of matzah
want to share a fruit slice?
next year in Jerusalem
let's do it again tomorrow night!

The Orchestra of Each

Each breath is a gale.
Each exhale a whisper.
Each hug is a spark.
Each idea a revelation.
Each sabbath is a song.
Each sukkah a shelter.
Each prayer is a wish.
Each embrace a longing.
Each morning is a revelation.
Each evening a chorus.
Each meeting is a potential.
Each love is a harmony.
Each smile is a wish.
Each human a maze.
Each beginning is an ending.
Each ending a beginning.
Each of you is a gift.

The Day After Yom Kippur

The day after Yom Kippur is a weird day.

You spend an entire day
pouring your heart out,
fasting, and asking forgiveness.

And then the next day it's back to life,
baseball games and Trader Joe's,
seeing the folks you just saw
at synagogue in the cereal aisle.

You made all these promises.
You said, I'll be better.
You are already back to old habits.

Yesterday feels like a dream.

So you close your eyes and breathe.
Remembering why you spent the day
tapping your heart and singing Avinu Malkeinu.

You realize you are who you are
and you are eternally growing.
You remember to forgive yourself
as you brush your teeth.

You watch a few more minutes
of Sunday football in bed before
turning off the TV and hearing the still small voice.

You set your alarm and drift to sleep.
You are forgiven.
You are beautiful.
Tomorrow begins anew.

Identity

The Song I Did Not Compose

I sing a song I did not compose.
I eat the fruit I did not grow.
I walk the trails I did not blaze.
I admire the tree I did not plant.

I eat the bread I did not bake.
I roam the earth I did not create.
I hum the prayer I did not write.
I play the strings I did not coil.

I carry a name I did not choose.
I inherited a story I did not write.
I received a world I did not design.
I carry a hope I did not kindle.

And for all of it, I am grateful.

It Was Never About

It was never about the four children,
but about seeing our children
for exactly who they are.

It was never about the four questions,
but about living with curiosity.

It was never about Dayenu,
but about going to sleep affirming
that today I was and I am enough.

It was never about the matzah,
but about acknowledging
the profound fragility of life.

It was never about the seder plate,
but about recognizing
the symbolism in everyday things.

It was never about the maggid,
but about asking our parents
to teach us their stories.

It was never about the saltwater,
but about giving space for tears.

It was never about the plagues,
but about recognizing where
our broken world needs us most.

It was never about the four cups,
but about embracing life's joys.

It was never about the seder,
but about seeking a sense
of order in a very chaotic world.

It was never about Elijah,
but about believing that
a better world is still possible.

It was never about the haggadah,
but about tradition telling us
that we each have a story to write.

It was, however, always about
the matzah ball soup.

My Magen

The Jewish star
I wear upon my neck
spoke to me tonight—

I need a break
I'm tired
it said in a huff.

So for the first time
since the October day
I took it off
and let it rest.

My magen,
my shield.

And there I stood,
bare.

Only then
could I see the
six points
of the star

in my eyes
that see beauty

in my heart
pointed Eastward

in my hands
repairing the world

in my feet
praying and marching

in my ears
listening to the cries

in my lips
reciting songs of peace.

And I will wear it,
always.

You are You

You are you
beautiful you
dancing free
we celebrate you
always you
nobody else
blessed you
you be you
there's nothing
like you believe
you me see
you are among
the most beautiful
of wild trees.

People of the Book

I ask Brous how to say amen,
and Kushner teaches me why
bad things happen to good people.

It is Held who shows me that
Judaism is about love
and Hoffman who welcomes me
into the age-old Jewish conversation.

I read Horn to grasp why
people only love dead Jews
and Hurwitz who helps me see
that we've been here all along.

I immerse in Tishby's guide to Israel
and Borowitz who uncovers
the masks that Jews wear.

Jacobs reveals to me why we are
obligated to pursue justice,
and Frankl who teaches me
on my search for meaning.

I seek Diamant in each moment
of the cycle of Jewish life
and Wiesel who reminds us all
to love and never be indifferent.

We are the people of the book.

People of Memory

We are a people of memory,
and everything is a reminder.
The kippah, a reminder to look up.
The candles, to know there is light.
The cup, to taste the sweetness.
The scroll, to lift up our story.
The spices, to always be fiery!
The menorah, to see the miracles.
The torn ribbon, to grieve.
The prayer shawl, to act justly.
The matzah, to repair the brokenness.
The shofar, to awaken our souls.
The star, to walk proudly.
The sukkah, to welcome the stranger.
The chuppah, to celebrate the joy.
The mezuzah, to mightily love.
The challah, to make two into one.
The sabbath, to quietly rest.
We are a people of memory,
and everything is a reminder.

Notes, Leaves, and Letters

I am but a stone in the streets of Jerusalem.
I am but a thread in the prayer shawl.
I am but a letter in the scrolls of Torah.
I am but a leaf in the tree of life.
I am but a name upon the wall of memory.
I am but a single word in every blessing.
I am but a sweet drop in the Kiddush cup.
I am but a note in the anthem of hope.
I am but a stitch in the wedding canopy.
I am but a braid in the havdalah candle.
I am but a small cry in the shofar blast.
I am but a voice in the song of peace.
And that is all I need to be.

New Years Affirmation

I am whole and I am unfinished.
I am wise and I am learning.
I am ready and I am unprepared.
I am body and I am breath.
I am speaking and I am listening.
I am my ancestors and I am my aspirations.
I am the earth and I am the sky.
I am a creator and I am a dismantler.
I am satisfied and I am restless.
I am the trees and I am the ocean.
I am courageous and I am afraid.
I am for myself and I am for you.
I am hopeful and I am deeply worried.
I am wandering and I am home.
I am beautiful and I am broken.
I am present and I am dreaming.
I am here and I am ready to enter.

God

I Scheduled a Meeting with God

I scheduled a morning meeting with God.
Subject: Role Clarification

God was five minutes early.
I was five minutes late.
My youngest missed the bus.

God seemed agitated.
What's this about?

Role clarification.
We humans feel like we're
shouldering a lot of the load
these days.
We need some help.

God burst into tears.
A daily occurrence.

You cover the earth.
I cover the sky.
Haven't we been over this?
God replied as She stared
out the window.

Well it's not working very well.
I replied as I tried to discern
what God was staring at.

God was silent for what
felt like an eternity.

(Continued)

I can't heal the sick.
Or stop wars.
I cannot prevent evil.
Or calm the seas.
I cannot change hearts.
Or bring peace.
I can pray for you.
And send angels to earth.
I can offer you strength.
And cry for you.
I can craft beautiful skies.
And incredible sunsets.
And I can believe in You.

Then I burst into tears.
A daily occurrence.

Divine Inhalations

As God inhales
the sun rises.

And as God exhales
the sun sets.

Waiting Up

God fell
asleep
on the
couch
again
for the
third time
this week.

She was
waiting up
for her
children
but they
were out
late
undoing
creation.

The angels
gently
carried God
up to bed
sitting by
Her side,
praying Her
children
would
return home
before dawn.

The Blessing of Uncertainty

I'm not certain there is a God,
but I live as though there is one.

I'm not certain there will ever be peace,
but I act with the belief it will come.

I'm not certain if there is truth,
but I ask questions hoping to find it.

I'm not certain the world is broken,
but I awake believing I can repair it.

I'm not certain of much of anything,
and thank goodness for that.

Loving Parent

Humanity
needs

a
loving
parent

right
now.

Blueprints for Eden

"Why are you
so surprised
by cruelty,"
God asked me
one night
over a beer.

"I don't
understand it,"
I replied
as I ate some fries.

"I created it.
And even I don't
understand it,"
said God.

"Maybe
we need to
eat from
the tree
once more,"
I said with bravery.

"To understand."
"Perhaps then…
you can
uncreate what
I created in error."

(Continued)

God's voice trailed off.
And then She was gone.
I was left
at a table for two,
alone

with the blueprints
for Eden.

Americanos with an Angel

On a sleepy island
just to the left of
a distant ocean tide

I saw the angel of peace
sipping an Americano
before the world awoke

and there I asked her
what she dreams about
as she sits by the sea

she told me she
dreams about the past
before the days of Eden

when the universe was
unformed and void
violent, ugly, and unruly

it was then one day God
called her from above
and asked for her help—

let us craft an earth
in our shared image:
my compassion, your peace

but it never came to be
as she handed me
the crumpled, unused plans

(Continued)

they're now yours, child
as she sipped her coffee
and gazed far beyond me

maybe you will succeed
where God and I could not
all those years ago.

I thanked her and left
as I floated away
into creation and possibility.

A Prayer for the Prayers

A prayer for the prayers
the words that get us through
we whisper them at night
or when reading the news.

Our prayers are our agency
our dust against the wind
a sentence of spirituality
a single pause in the chaos.

Each prayer from experience
from losing and grieving
sent via air mail to heaven
or across the wild earth.

I imagine our prayers
dancing towards the sky
held on by a thread
to us and to the divine.

Prayers are more than
a book, a hymnal or page
they are all we may have
on our most difficult days.

The Annual Chanukah Party

God canceled the annual Chanukah party.
Too many of God's children suffering.
Too much of God's earth wilting.

The angels showed up anyways.
They brought latkes and dreidels,
jelly donuts and a glimmering menorah.

Your children sing of Your wonders
as they kindle the festival lights!
They will surely find their way again.

It will take a miracle, replied God.
Exactly, sang the angels. Exactly.

Refunds

I waited in line for hours.
Finally I reached the desk.
I want a refund, I said.
For what?
All my prayers for peace.

I'm sorry I don't really do refunds.
But you're God you can do anything.
Who told you that?
I read it somewhere.

Those prayers aren't for me.
Yes they are.
They're for you.
Well either way they don't work.

Maybe we should sing together.
So I sang the prayer for peace with God.
We both cried.

And then I went home,
still hearing God singing
a prayer, for peace, for us.

Trick or Treat

I went out trick or treating.
I saw God dressed up as a human
and I was dressed up as God.

When we saw each other
we cried and shed our masks
sharing a much needed embrace.

We promised to stay in touch
as children walked past
and God disappeared away.

P.S. God likes Kit Kats.

God the Painter

God likes to paint the walls
with vivid bright colors
every afternoon around 4—
with fluorescent greens
cotton candy pinks
blueberry blues and
purples off the vine.

God is a wonder of color
majestic artistic creativity
transforming bare walls
into a modern museum
of ancestral art,
each wave of the paintbrush
a return to Eden's gardens.

As evening mixes in
the colors disappear
like fog upon a bridge
narrowing into the dark,
the beautiful painting
remains in my memory
as I kiss the world goodnight.

Desire

I Don't Want to be Heartless

I left my heart
on a park bench,
so I could run free
through the flowering fields.

When I returned
my heart was gone,
I could hear its beat
in the distant trees.

I don't want to be heartless!
Like those who turn their backs
on the hungry and the tired
I cried and I cried.

And then I awoke—
clenching my beating heart,
cherishing its burden and fullness
right there, within me.

The Foolish Builder

Perhaps
the ships of war
will always
knock down
the fragile
bridges of peace.

And perhaps
in foolishness,
I will perpetually
keep trying
to build them.

Psalm 151

I'm waiting for
a beautiful soul
to write the words
of psalm 151
for my lute and lyre
are long put away
and my people
are in need of
a psalmist today
to speak the words
the ancients
could not say.

Tradition…tradition!
the Hebrew word
for tradition,
masoret מסורת,
has not one,
but two
Hebrew roots.

The root
alef-samech-resh
means
to bind
to tie up
to imprison.

(Continued)

And the root
mem-samech-resh
means
to pass down
to transfer
to deliver.

So please understand
part of who I am was
chosen for me
and part each day
I choose to be.

Keep Singing

I knelt beside the sacred tree
her bark so fragile, injured, and torn
by rockets, rocks, and distant haze.

She asked me with a willowed voice
to play her the sweetest of songs,
"a song that heals my ancient soul."

And as her leaves and wild flowers
tiptoed gracefully to the rocky earth
I sang a song I learned in Jerusalem.

A familiar song, a hopeless song,
a Jewish song, a hope filled song,
a missing song, a wishful song.

And when I stood up to return to war
I left that song at the foot of the tree
and asked her to keep singing it, for me.

Yerushalmi Poems

I want to build a sukkah
made of bricks and of stones
where I can sit and sing
and read Yerushalmi poems.

Sheltered from the world
in my fortified hut
the wars and the hurricanes
my tired soul would be shut.

I would slowly forget
as the days passed on by
who the stars resemble
and what makes me cry.

One will never find peace
in a sukkah of stone
only with branches and leaves
can one truly be home.

The Prophetess and the Poetess

Miriam the
Prophetess
met
Emma Lazarus
the Poetess

at a protest march.

The two met
every day thereafter.

Miriam danced.
Emma wrote.

Miriam sang.
Emma composed.

Miriam was like water.
Emma, like fire.

They became like one.
As a braided candle.

But then God
split them apart—
like the seas

for they were
too powerful
and free.

(Continued)

And each day since,
the world would pray

that the prophetess
and the poetess
will again become one.

About the Author

RABBI EVAN SCHULTZ, author of *Morning, Noon, and Night: Poetry in the Language of Jewish Time*, serves as Senior Rabbi of Congregation B'nai Israel in Bridgeport, Connecticut. His writings have been featured on Kveller.com and thewisdomdaily.com, as well as in such publications as *The Times of Israel*. He lives in Connecticut with his wife, Jenny, and their three children.

Follow Rabbi Schultz on instagram @barefoot_rabbi

www.ingramcontent.com/pod-product-compliance
Lightning Source LLC
Chambersburg PA
CBHW020243010526
44107CB00002B/80